VACANT LOT, SCHOOL YARD, AND BACK ALLEY GAMES

Bodman, Jackie

Boka, Brian

Bonnichsen, Stephani

Bunn, Joe

Fultz, Tracy

Gage, Melissa

Haag, Bart

Langstaff, Sam

Lessenger, Amberly

Lorber, Lindsey

McGill, Mike

Miller, Jennifer

Mohror, Katie

Noll, Garren

Wilson, Mike

Wilson, Rebecca Erwin

QUIXOTE PRESS
R.R. #4, Box 33B
Blvd. Station
Sioux City, Iowa
51109

* * * * * * * * *

QUIXOTE
PRESS
Bruce Carlson
R.R. #4, Box 33B
Blvd. Station
Sioux City, Iowa
51109

PRINTED
IN
U.S.A.

iii

DEDICATION

—to all the children of yesterday
and today.

Table of Contents

FOREWORD

What is it about the games that children play, and those they played years ago when the trials and tribulations of adulthood weren't really part of reality?

What is it that makes those silly little things with their "It's" and their counting and eye hiding part of our lives we never really get over?

We can take trips to California and find it isn't like we thought it would be, or Dublin or Rio. But our quiet little trips back to our childhood always show us a land as we knew it to be.

How many of us can hear the words ". . . . . . . 7-8-9-10, Here I come, ready or not.", without remembering how we had to fight to hold our breath quiet so the "It" wouldn't find us behind the lilac bush? . . . . or under that pile of leaves that Dad had raked up just that afternoon?

Prof. Phil Hey
Briar Cliff College
Sioux City, Ia.

PREFACE

These accounts of the games that the children of America's Heartland played years and years ago are not profound cultural entities.

They aren't things that make the world go around or set the course of events for mankind.

.... or are they?

I

INDIAN RUNNING

his game is played in the school classroom because it's supposed to be a quiet game. Probably, though, there are many teachers of years ago who wouldn't have called it that.

Five or six players are picked to go out of the room. These players arrange themselves in any order. They then come back into the room, running around it once and quickly leave again.

The first one of those remaining in the classroom who names all the incoming ones in correct order gets to pick five other players and they all start over again.

To make the game a little tougher, the pupils may have more runners or have to name the runners in correct order and then follow that up by saying

the name of a city, state, or animal beginning with the same letter of the alphabet as each runner's name.

This game was played by my great aunt and her classmates in Lacon, Illinois, a little town nestled along the Illinois River.

—*Jennifer Miller*

II

PASTE TAG

aste tag was played in lots of one room schools. The setting was good for this game because student desks were connected together in rows. That made for nice wide aisles for running.

Someone was chosen to be the "IT".

Two children were chosen to run down separate aisles to a table in the front of the room where the paste jar would be setting on that table.

The object of the game was to see which one could could get to the jar before being tagged by the "IT". If a player was tagged, then he or she became the new "IT".

(15)

My mother and her friend, Katherine were racing for the paste jar when, as Katherine grabbed the jar, the lid flipped off. Somehow the jar went flying up in the air. When it came down again it did so right on Katherine, getting in her hair, on her face and all over her dress.

The kids, of course, had all kinds of fun watching poor Katherine try to figure out what happened, and why.

Of course, it was THOSE BOYS, who had the most fun out of it.

Mom said that she didn't really mind losing that round of Paste Tag since her friend got into such a mess.

—*Amberly Lessenger*

III

ERASER RELAY

o play eraser relay, all children stay in their seats. Each row across the width of the room makes up one of the teams.

A clean eraser is put on the floor in the outside aisle beside the first desk in each cross row.

On the command, "GO", each child in the first seat picks up the eraser assigned to that team, and puts it on the floor to the left. The next student grabs it in his right hand, and moves it over to the floor to his left.

And, so the process goes across the width of the room, accompained, of course, by all sorts of shrieks and shouts.

The row that wins is the first one that gets their eraser all the way over, laying on the floor to the left of the far left pupil.

The teacher or one of the older pupils would get to sit up in front to judge as to who's eraser got there first.

My Dad, James Wilson, remembers playing ERASER RELAY during many indoor recesses at the rural Hopewell School in Port Louisa Township.

—*Mike Wilson*

IV

THIS IS THE WAY

 ome times, when the children would first get to school on a winter morning, they would find the old potbellied hadn't really warmed the room up very well yet.

But, there was an answer to that. They would play THIS IS THE WAY.

The children would sing, "This is the way we clap our hands, clap our hands, clap our hands, this is the way we clap our hands so early in the morning."

As they sang, they would do what the song said. This game continued with other verses like "This is the way we stomp our feet," and so on.

It was during that "feet stompin" part that little Fredrick got in trouble. He played so enthusiastically that he stomped all the old dried mud off of his shoes onto the floor.

Since the teacher was also the janitor, she didn't think that was the least bit funny, and figured Fredrick did it on purpose.

So, Fredrick got to stay after school, clean up the floor, and the rest of the room also.

To make matters worse for Fredrick, when his Pa found out the young lad got into trouble at school he made Fredrick clean out the chicken house that night.

The next time the class played "This is the Way," Fredrick must have learned his lesson because he just stood quietly when it came to the foot stompin' part.

—*Jennifer Miller*

V

BUMPETY BUMP BUMP

t takes a lot of people to play the game of Bumpety Bump Bump. Fifteen or twenty is a good number, so it would usually take the whole school to get such a game going.

The players sit or stand in a circle. One player is put in the middle. If a real large group is playing, there might be several players in the center.

A center person moves around in a circle, then points at someone and says, "Right Bumpety Bump Bump, 1-2-3-4-5-6-7-8-9-10."

Before the person reaches ten the player who got pointed at has to say the person's name to his or her right. If the player doesn't say the name, he is now the center person.

It is the same for left. The person in the center says, "Left, Bumpty Bump Bump."

Then, of course, the person in the circle has to give the name of the person on his left.

Sometimes the kids would get so confused that they would hardly know their own name, much less that of their neighbor.

—*Lindsey Lorber*

VI

RITES OF PASSAGE

ith this printing, the secret is out. If any of you readers graduated from the eighth grade at Carson School in Louisa County, you already know about this.

The boys going through that school somehow developed their own "Rite of Passage". Many believe it all began with a dare.

As the story goes, before any eighth grade boy could leave Carson School, he was obliged to carve his initials somewhere in the slate chalkboard.

Of course, that had to be done without the teacher finding out about it.

It was really tough to pull this off because the teacher almost never left the room without the students. About the only time was when she would, to go to the outhouse.

While the teacher was thus occupied, the boys would stand guard for each other, and signal when she started coming back down that well-worn path to the schoolhouse.

More times than once, the young sculptor would find it necessary to skin on out an open window and casually join the others at recess.

—*The Kids*

VII

CUPS

UPS can be played by two or more people.

Each player must wear a handerchief in his back pocket and have two or more cups apiece.

Then a line is drawn in the middle of the playing area and players divide equally on each side of the line. The same number of cups are put at the back boundries of each side.

The object of the game is for the players to run across the line, steal one cup at a time and take it back to where their own cups are, without someone on the other side grabbing the hankerchief from their back pocket.

When someone grabs the hanky before its owner gets back to the safe side, the cup has to be returned to its side. The game goes on until one side has all the cups.

This game is believed to have gotten started years ago at Kilpeck Landing when two children went out to feed their cats and found they had only one cup, when they needed two, one for each cat.

Between the children playfully stealing that cup from each other, and one grabbing the other's hankie in retaliation, they invented the game right there while they were doing their chores.

—*Stephani Bonnichsen*

VIII

ICE BLOCK SLIDING

y father, Steve Boka, grew up in Clinton, Iowa. Every time we go there to visit, he always tells me stories about when he was a kid. My favorite is the one about when the and his friends would do what they called "ice block sliding."

It was the last day of school and the temperature was in the 90's. The children had been negotiating

for weeks with their teacher, Mrs. Krueger, for an end-of-the-school-year ice block sliding party. As it turned out, everyone got a "B" or better on their spelling test so the party was going to happen.

At noon recess, Father and two of his friends were given permission to walk down to the gas station called "The Ice House". That was where they sold beautiful sparkly blocks of ice that always looked kind of special in the heat of the summer.

They made their chilly purchase and staggered back to school bearing that cold slippery block of Ice. Their school was on top of a long hill, a perfect place for both ice block sliding and winter sledding as well.

The party started as soon as the boys got back, for it was a race with the heat of the day to make as many trips as possible down that hill.

When my father first told me about ice block sliding, he was going fifteen miles an hour down the hill. The last time I heard it, it was up to 65.

—*Brian Boka*

IX

THE HOMEMADE TOY

he toys and pasttimes of the country children in the 1920's and 30's were different than what kids play with today. The hard times kept store bought toys out of the hands of children, but put ideas for home-made ones in their heads. The children were always inventing toys from thrown away things on hand.

So it was with little Carey Idell Erwin who remembers playing at her childhood home in Bible Grove, Missouri, near the Fabius River in Scotland County.

Carey and the other children learned they could have a lot of fun putting their hands and heads to work on their playthings.

One of the things they would do was to take the rim off of an old iron-rimmed wooden wheel. Once freed of the rest of the wheel, the rim proved to be a twelve to fourteen inch hoop that could be made into lots of things.

One of these things was a rolling hoop. With a stick to guide it, the children found they could run that hoop all over, running along side it, watching the magic of the iron rim as it seemed to come alive on a idle summer day.

—*The Kids*

X

EARSIES-NOSIES

ll players form a circle facing toward the center in this old fashioned game. One of the group is the "IT", and stands in the center.

The "IT" will call out the name of one of the other players. The one whose name is called, has to hold on to both of his ears.

Then, the person on the right of the ear holder has to hold onto his left ear and his nose. The person on the left has to hold onto his right ear and his nose.

(31)

The one who is the slowest is doing all that is judged to be the new "IT".

My Grandma played Earsies-Nosies back when she was a child growing up in Rock Island, Illinois. She especially remembers one time when her oldest brother, Tom, had been working on their father's car, and joined the game late.

Tom was standing next to Jake, their other brother, when the "IT" called Jake's name. Tom, of course, had to grab his nose and left ear. At this everyone started to laugh loudly.

Tom, not knowing what was happening, started to get mad about it all until someone told him about the black grimy grease all over his nose.

—*Jennifer Miller*

XI

RIDING DOWN TREES

y Mother has often talked about growing up in the years of The Great Depression. Some of her reflections include her getting only a single hair ribbon for Christmas one year and eating only wild rabbit all winter because there was no other meat to be had.

And, if food was hard to come by, toys were even harder. Whatever the children played with, they made themselves.

One of the favorite past-times for the neighborhood kids was riding down trees in the woods.

First they had to choose a small tree with bendable limbs. Next, each rider would climb his tree, and grab hold of the far end of one of the limbs. Then, hanging on for dear life, they'd jump out of the tree.

A well chosen limb offered just enough support to let them down gently to the ground. One too limber would teach a kid all he wanted to know about the fun of having the "wind knocked out of him."

Sometimes in the late spring when the creeks were swollen, the kids would ride down trees into the water. The one who could ride down the biggest tree would be declared the winner for the day.

Children from all over Northeast Missouri spent many hours entertaining themselves in those times of few toys.

—*Becky Wilson*

XII

BOXES

oxes can be played with two or more players. Before starting the game, make a grid of dots in a vertical and horizontal pattern.

To start the game, one player draws a line connecting two dots. The object of the game is for each player to take turns connecting dots to

make square boxes. The person drawing the fourth line to complete a box got to put his initials inside that box. The one who has their initials in the most boxes at the end of the game is the winner.

(35)

Most of the time this game is played by using paper and pencil or the chalkboard for making the grid.

One time the Langston children were camping with their parents at their cabin on the Mississippi River near Hannibal, Missouri.

After the fishing, swimming and the evening weiner roast, the children began a game of boxes in the sand. They used sticks to make the grid of dots and lines in the sand.

Before the children finished the game, darkness set in, forcing the kids inside the cabin to get ready for bed. The children really hated to stop playing because they were tied with seven squares each.

The desire to win called the children back to finish the game after breakfast the next morning.

Much to their surprise, the sand grid looked like some sort of Etyptian hieroglyphics. There were funny lines all over their game and even down to the water's edge.

The two of them came rushing back to the cabin, telling of how some sort of monster must have come during the night to destroy their boxes game.

They told of how this monster must have messed up their game and how he must have been a jillion feet tall and probably ate campers for breakfast.

After showing the grown-ups the evidence of the monster having been there in the night, one of the grown-ups figured that it probably wasn't a monster at all. He figured it might be more like some hungry raccoon who was probably just after their discarded hunks of hot dogs and buns . . . . . . or maybe the critter simply wanted to play "boxes".

—Bart Haag

XIII

TIDDLY WINKS

iddly Winks is a simple game enjoyed by children years ago as well as today.

Things needed to play the game are: one large round flat object (the shooter), five smaller round fat objects (the chips), and a cup or other container to be the goal.

To start playing, the shooter is pressed on the edge of one of the small chips. The chip will flip up into the air when you bear down with the shooter. The player tries to aim so that the chip will land in the cup. If the chip makes it into the cup, that player gets two points.

Each player shoots all five chips and gets two tries per chip. When he is done, the other players get their turn. A total score is kept until the players decide to stop.

Tiddly Winks can be purchased at stores today, but years ago children used a variety of things to play the game.

One lady recalls that she and her friends would sometimes use Mason flats and tins of one kind or another just to make a novel kind of tiddly winks game.

—*Bart Haag*

XIV

STATUE TAG

s a child, my great grandpa used to play statue tag with his friends in Alamakee County, Iowa. He lived in a little town called Harper's Ferry, along the river. Back in those days the kids of Harper's Ferry spent most of their free time with outdoor games or water fun.

To play Statue Tag, you need four or more players. One person is the store owner, one person is the shopper, and two or more people are the statues in the store.

The shopper comes in and tells the store owner he wants to buy a statue. The store owner takes the shopper around to various satues.

At this time, the statue people do actions like they are somebody different than themselves. They may act like they are a cook, an acrobat, an Indian warrior or whatever they want.

The shopper guesses who they are acting out. If the shopper guesses correctly, everybody rotates to a different part and the game starts all over again. If the shopper can't guess correctly, each player's part stays the same.

—*Amberly Lessenger*

XV

FOX AND GOOSE

To play the game you need three or more players and a big snowy area.

First you trample down a large circle in the snow, then trample lines so as to divide the circle into fourths and then again divide each of those sections in half, making eighths. Next, it is necessary to trample down another circle in the very center of the large one.

This is followed by one more circle, about half way the size of the largest one, and made between the large one and the center one. These circles are the paths for the fox and the geese.

There is but one fox chosen from among the children, and the rest are geese. The fox and the geese must stay in the trampled lines in the snow and have to drop out of the game if they don't.

The idea is for the geese to get to the very middle circle without being tagged by the fox. But, the geese can only be in the safe center circle for five seconds before they have to run out again.

The fox is allowed to go through the center in his effort to catch a goose except when there is a goose in that safe position. If there is a goose in the center, the fox has to run around another way to tag one of the other geese.

My grandfather played this game when he was a

(44)

small boy, growing up on their family farm along the Mississippi River. Grandpa recalled how delicious cookies and hot chocolate could be after a vigorous game of Fox and Goose.

—Tracy Fultz

XVI

MIDNIGHT

 idnight is played with three or more players. It is a fun game that can be played either outside or in a big enclosed area.

First of all, some object is chosen as the base, and one of the players is chosen to be "IT". Very often the base is a corner of a building or a tree.

The "IT" person walks to the opposite side of the yard or play area away from the other players and turns his back to them.

All the rest of the players stand near the tree or whatever else is base and yell, "What time is it, Mister Clock?"

The "IT" then says the time, for example, Nine O'Clock. This would be the signal for the other players to take nine steps across the field toward the "IT".

The question is repeated with the "IT" saying different times as the players respond by taking that many steps.

When the "IT" thinks the other players are close, he yells, "Midnight", turns, and chases the others back to the base. If someone is caught, that person becomes the new "IT".

(48)

In Dubuque, Iowa, back in the early '50s, the children used to pick the old corner lamp posts for base. Those posts lighted the red brick streets of the city back in those days.

A favorite spot was a sand lot near the meat packing plant. Dubuque children living in the neighborhood would gather in the lot after school, play Midnight, then walk or ride home with their fathers when their shift ended at the plant.

—Jackie Bodman

XVII

ERASER TAG

y mother played this game in grade school on rainy or very cold days when they had to stay inside for recess.

The game would start out with only two people playing, the rest of the students sitting in their seats.

Both of the people playing would balance a blackboard eraser on their heads.

The object of the game was for each person to try to touch the other person without getting touched himself, or letting the eraser fall off of his own head. If the eraser came off, or if someone touched you, you would have to sit down and pick another student to take your place.

Mother said that sometimes the kids would pick the teacher to take their place.

She said she could still picture her teacher running around with an eraser on her head, trying to run in her high heel shoes.

One time when the teacher was trying to do that she stumbled and the eraser fell off of her head, landing right on the head of John Raymond. John was a fifth grader. When it hit him the chalk dust came raisin' up like a big old dirt cloud on a dirt road when a car goes by real fast.

John got to jumpin' around trying' to get rid of all that chalk dust, and the more he slapped on his clothing to get shed of that white stuff, the more of it came flyin' up out of his clothes into the air, makin' him and the teacher choke and gasp something awful.

By the time things got settled down, poor little Johnny Raymond looked like an old man with real grey hair and the teacher looked like she'd been in a rassle fight with a big dog.

The next class was Georgraphy class, but everyone got to laughing so hard over what had happened

GEOGRAPHY

that they had a hard time getting very interested in Geography.

—*Jennifer Miller*

XVIII

RED LIGHT, GREEN LIGHT

ny number of students can play this game that was so popular years ago.

One student is picked out to be the traffic light. Another stands with his back to the other players. He then shouts "Green Light" which lets the other children move forward toward him until he shouts out "Red Light."

The traffic light then whirls around real fast to see if he can catch any of the other students still moving. And, anyone he catches still moving has to go back to the starting line to start all over again.

The game goes on until one of the students reaches the area past the Traffic Light. When that happens, the game is over with.

At the end of that round, a new Traffic Light is selected, and a whole new round starts again.

—*Stephani Bonnichsen*

XIX

THREE DEEP

 ne player is chose as the runner and another is "IT". The remaining players stand in a double circle, and facing the center of the circle. The one who is "IT" chases the runner, who is safe by stepping in front of any couple in the circle.

When that happens the outside player of that couple becomes the new runner, and the game continues.

Whenever a runner is tagged, he becomes the new "IT" and the player who tagged him becomes the new runner.

If the children who are playing are older the game can be made more challenging by not allowing players to cut across the circle. They must go around the outside of the circle.

Three Deep was a popular game on most all school playgrounds years ago. Probably no more fun playing this game was had anywhere than that enjoyed by the children of Elsberry Missouri. They would even play it in the dark and make a very large circle to add more challenge and excitement.

—The Kids

XX

BLIND MAN'S BLUFF

o play Blind Man's Bluff you need a blindfold and six or more players. One of the players is chosen to be blindfolded. Then he is spun around and around.

The rest of the players scatter all over the place. It makes it more fun when people come up and tease the blind man and duck away.

When the blind man touches one of the players, the person touched becomes the new blindman. The old blind man takes off the blindfold and becomes one of the players.

The game continues until everyone gets tired of playing or until recess is over.

My grandma, Ethel, was the worst player of all. It took a half an hour or more for her just to touch another person.

Everyone always tried to get right in front of her so the game would get over with quicker.

Grandma and her friends in Decorah, Iowa spent endless hours playing this game along the banks of the Upper Iowa River.

—*Lindsey Lorber*

XXI

HIDE THE BONE

his game is much like Button-Button. To play Hide the Bone you need a small object that can be hidden in your hand, like a pen or paper clip, and at least five people are needed to play.

The group picks one person to be "IT" and another person to be the "dog". Everybody else sits in a circle and the "dog" steps out of the room or hides his eyes in a corner facing away from the circle. The person who is "IT" then comes around the circle and pretends to give the bone to everyone in the circle.

But, he really only gives it to one person although everyone in turn pretends to take it. When the "IT" is done making his rounds, everybody calls out, "Doggie, Doggie, who's got the bone?" Then the dog comes out and guesses who had the "bone" hidden in their hands. The "dog" gets two guesses.

If he guesses correctly, then he has the privilege of being the "dog" for another round. If he doesn't guess correctly within two guesses, his first guess gets to be the "dog". A different person is "IT" each time.

I learned this game from my mother who remembers playing it as a young girl in the Minnesota Twin Cities.

Amanda, one of Mother's classmates, could always seem to guess who had the bone. She was especially good at looking people in the eye and reading their thoughts. Sometimes she would make whoever had the bone get to laughing, just by starting at them. Because she was able to do this, she would sometimes be the dog for almost the entire game.

—*Tracy Fultz*

XXII

RED ROVER

wo lines of any number of children holding hands stand parallel to each other. These are the two teams. One of the teams yells, "Red Rover, red rover, send . . . . right over." (They say the name of a person on the other team.)

The person whose name is called runs and chooses two joined hands to break through. If the person breaks through, he gets to choose one person from the opposing team to take back to his own team.

If, however, he didn't break through he had to join that team.

You win when the whole opposing team is on your side. The first team to get all of the opposite team on its side is declared the winner.

My teacher, Ms. Jackson, remembers, with some pain, her last experience playing Red Rover. It was at morning recess in 1958 at the Novelty Community School in Novelty, Missouri. There was some dew on the grass and only two people left on the opposing team. She was called to run over. In the process, she broke through their joined hands, but slipped on the wet grass. She fell, and broke her right arm.

—Sam Langstaff

XXIII

CLOTHES PIN DROP

ou can use one or more players in this game. All you'll need is a gallon or quart jar and the clothes pins.

Get a high backed chair and face it backwards to the bottle that is placed on the floor no more than two feet away from the chair.

Kneel on your knees in the chair. Rest your hand on the back of the chair with one pin held in your fingers.

Next, aim at the hole on the top of the bottle and drop the pin. If you don't make the first one, you still have nine more pins to go.

You get one point for each pin that you manage to drop into the open mouth of the bottle.

(65)

My mother remembers playing this game when she was growing up. Mother and her friends played

it at birthday parties and on rainy days when they couldn't go outside and play those games where they could run and shout.

—*Lindsey Lorber*

XXIV

UMBRELLA FANTASY

other and Aunt Vergie were quite the pair! As kids back in the 1930s, they could dream up some of the dangest things. What one didn't think of, the other did. Grandma used to say that they had the imagination of ten kids put together.

One July morning the girls woke up to the crowing of Grandma's old rooster. After eating their breakfast of side pork and eggs, the pair set out for adventures.

Aunt Vergie spied Grandma's old black umbrella by the back door. With Mother looking on Vergie, stepped out the door and started to toss it into the air to see if it would drift to the ground like a parachute.

It looked like it might work, so the next step was to experiment from the hay loft. Since Aunt Vergie was three years older than Mother she had a way of influencing her little cousin to do things she shouldn't have. Mother was simply an innocent victim.

With the umbrella in hand, Mother, at the count of three, jumped from the loft toward the ground far below.

She dropped like a bale of straw, landing on both feet alright, but biting her tongue as her chin slammed into her knee.

I can picture it all now. Aunt Vergie was laughing at the comic scene while running to the house for protection behind Grandma's apron.

Aunt Vergie is gone now, but Mother still laughs when reminiscing about some of the things they did as children. When I asked her if she ever got back at Vergie, Mom said, "No, not really. I loved her too much."

—Becky Wilson

XXV

NICE KITTY

ne person, "the kitten", goes around a circle of children. This person who is "IT" stops and stands face to face with someone in the circle and says, "Meow" three times without laughing. Then that person stands up and says "Nice Kitty" three times, also without laughing. Whichever laughs or even smiles has to be the new kitten.

My mother remembers that there was one girl in our class that would never laugh. She always won, and wasn't a whole lot of fun to play with.

Mother said she can remember only one time when that girl laughed. That was a time when a real kitty came out from behind a lilac bush meowing. It must have heard the children meowing while playing the game.

This game was played only by the girls. It seemed to be a real challenge to them since they were always so giggly they found it hard not to break out into giggles just thinking about the game.

The boys mostly played baseball at recess, but would often tease the girls by yelling over to them "Meow, Meow, Kitty, Kitty."

Sometimes when the teacher would decide what the children would play at recess, the girls would get her to make the boys play NICE KITTY, too.

—*Jennifer Miller*

XXVI

SIMON SAYS

IMON SAYS was a game played and enjoyed by children in the past.

To play the game you pick a leader or a "Simon" and then that person then says, for example, "Simon says, . . . Hit yourself in the head." Then all the other players would do so. But, if the Simon, just said, "Hit yourself in the head" without the word Simon in front of it, you aren't supposed to perform the thing. If anyone goes ahead and does it, that person is out of the game. The last person left, that followed all of Simon's commands and hadn't been tricked, becomes the new Simon.

One time, back in 1946, Ethel a lady in my neighborhood in Grandview, Iowa, was playing Simon Says with her grandpa.

She was Simon and gave the command, "Simon says . . . Pull your hair."

This lady's grandpa's mouth dropped open and he looked at her funny. He said "You win!"

For, you see, her Grandpa was as bald as he could be.

—*Mike McGill*

XXVII

DUCK, DUCK, GOOSE

his game is very similar to "Drop the Handerchief". The "ducks" sit in a circle while the "goose" moves around in a circle behind them.

As the "goose" makes his rounds he taps each player on the head, and in so doing, says the words "duck". Each player then ducks his head when tapped.

When the "goose" touches one of the players and says "goose" he runs as fast as he can around the circle with the new "goose" trying to catch him. The old "goose" tries to reach the spot where the new "goose" was sitting before being tagged.

If he's caught, he has to sit inside the circle and stay there until another player is caught at which time they exchange places.

The children of Letts and Columbus Junction in Iowa loved to play this game back in the 1940's.

Katie Mohror

XXVIII

WHIRL A BUTTON

HIRL-A-BUTTON is a solitary game. It was originally made up for poor children to pass the time away. All that's needed is a button and a piece of string or thread.

You thread the thread or string through a two or four hole button and tie the ends together. You have to be sure that the two sides of the loop go through different holes in the button instead of through the same one.

Next, you take your two index fingers and slip them into the loops formed by the string. Rotate the button until the string is somewhat twisted. This twisting shortens the string, drawing the fingers toward the center.

By pulling the fingers apart, the string rapidly untwists, then twists up again, but in the oppostite direction which again draws the fingers in together. The twisting and untwisting of the string causes it to behave much like elastic as it seems to stretch in and out. If you twist the string too tightly, it can pinch your fingers.

My grandma showed me how to make this simple game as her mother had taught her. Back when Grandma was a child, families had little money for buying games in stores. This one really costs nothing to make and is a lot of fun to play.

—*Katie Mohror*

XXIX

HOPSCOTCH

he rules for the game are that each player has to find her own rock. They can use chalk or a lime rock to draw the numbers in squares from one to ten, on the sidewalk.

Then, the players throw their rocks onto the numbered squares. Whichever square it lands on is designated the "miss" square for that game. The player tries to bypass the rock square while jumping the numbers in order from one to ten.

After going through the course once, players would turn and jump the squares in reverse order. While jumping back she must stop, pick up the rock, and proceed back to the original starting point.

My great aunt Nellie told me about the fun and fright she and her cousin Edith had while playing hopscotch in the summer of 1942. They were at their Uncle Arthur's place south of Mount Pleasant, Iowa along the Skunk River.

(77)

The girls had become bored with picking wild flowers along the bank and quickly became attracted to an old wooden bridge that went over a small creek running into the river.

Years earlier, the bridge had been used to move machinery from one side to the other.

Such an attraction couldn't be resisted. It was only a matter of minutes until the girls sketched their hopscotch pattern on what looked like good sound boards.

But, for Nellie, it was a hop, a skip, and a plunge to the creek bed below when a board gave way. Luckily, Nellie got out of that with only a scrape on her leg.

The girls did learn, however, not to play on rotten old bridges anymore.

—*Melissa Gage*

XXX

SHEEP'S IN, SHEEP'S OUT

o play Sheep's In, you must have six or more players and a designated tree or object to be the "Sheep's Pen".

A stick is laid by the sheep's pen as one player who is "IT" counts while the other players, or sheep, hide. After the person who is "IT" is done counting he goes out to try to find

the other players. Each player, whose name is called, must return to the pen as "captured" sheep. If one of the "sheep" reaches the sheep's pen without being seen, that person throws the stick out and yells, "Sheep's out!" All the other players run to hide once again. The game is over when all players are in the sheep's pen.

In 1957 some of the kids were playing the game at Humphrey, Iowa. On this particular day the grass was about waist high to the kids. That made it easier for the sheep to hide, but harder for them to find the stick.

The game had been going a while. Fred was "IT", and a huge oak tree was the base or sheep's pen. Tom was really good at sneaking up and throwing the stick to let the sheep out.

This time, though, when Tom came up from behind the big oak and reached to grab the stick he found that Fred had put it on top of a dead smelly skunk. Tom wasn't about to touch it, so Fred declared himself the winner.

—Garren Noll

XXXI

TWO SQUARE & FOUR SQUARE

ll you need to play two square is a basketball. You have to find a line or a crack in the sidewalk or pavement.

Sometimes kids would take a piece of chalk and draw their own line.

One person hits the ball across the line to the other person. That player must then let it bounce only once before they hit it back across the line to the first player. They continue this until someone goes out. A person goes out by letting the ball hit twice, catching it, or hitting it out of bounds.

This game can be played with four squares or with the two squares and three players with one rotating in when a person gets out.

Two squares has been played by kids for years. Nellie, a neighbor lady, told me about playing the game as a child after church on Sundays.

(81)

She and her cousin would sneak out behind the outhouse, make a line in the dirt with a stick, and play two-square while their parents were visiting with other people in the church. When Nellie's father would call her name, the girls would hide the weathered old ball in the lilac bushes and run to join their parents. Unknown to their folks, the girls enjoyed many games of two-square out behind that old outhouse.

—*Joe Bunn*

XXXII

PIN THE TAIL ON THE DONKEY

t was the night of my eleventh birthday party. My friends and I had eaten all the pizza, drank all the pop, and played all the games we could think of. Things were starting to get a bit dull!

Then the phone rang, it was my Uncle Jim calling to wish me a happy birthday. I told him that we needed an idea for another game to play.

Uncle Jim suggested that we play an old game called "Pin The Tail On The Donkey."

After Uncle Jim explained to me how to draw the south end of a donkey, how to make the tails, and what to use as a blindfold, we started to play.

(83)

Lucy wanted to go first. So, we blindfolded her, handed her a pin and a tail with her name on it, twirled her around, and then told her to pin the tail on the donkey.

My brother hadn't been taking part of the fun very much, or acting very interested in what was going on. But that stopped real quick when Lucy started to pin that donkey tail right on the back of his head.

—*Stephani Bonnichsen*

XXXIII

TOSS THE FEATHER

irst, every player gets seven long feathers. They should be about as much alike as possible.

A particular tree is picked out as the target. One person starts by throwing one of their feathers at the tree while they're standing behind a line about six paces from the tree.

The next person takes his place behind the line in the dirt and throws his feather. This goes on until everyone has thrown all of his feathers.

The person whose feather lands nearest the tree wins that round.

The process is repeated over and over until all seven feathers have been thrown.

Years ago, my grandmother used to play Toss the Feather after Sunday dinner with her cousins.

If they couldn't find enough feathers in the chicken yard they would have to separate a feather from one of the chickens. This would often earn the girls a few good hard pecks from the chicken or a spanking from one of the grown-ups. Sometimes they'd get both a good pecking and a spanking.

The girls thought that a few chicken pecks, or even a spanking, wasn't too high a price to pay for a good game. But, they agreed, when they got both, it simply wasn't worth the trouble.

—*Jennifer Miller*

XXXIV

CHARADES

o begin a game of Charades, two teams are chosen. Then one team brainstorms up a picture, word, or phrase to be acted out without talking.

That team then acts it out while the other team tries to guess what it is they are doing; all in a certain amount of time.

If the guessing team gets it within the time, they get a point. If the time runs out without a correct guess, the acting team gets the point.

(87)

The teams take turns acting out and guessing. The one with the most points when they quit playing is the winning team.

One night when my mother was a girl, she had a slumber party. She and the five girls staying with her, played charades half the night.

They imitated teachers, boys in their class, and scarey things. This led them to telling ghost stories, makin' them all scared half to death. They slept that night with the lights on.

—*Bart Haag*

XXXV

HIDE THE THIMBLE

ide The Thimble is an old game, played a lot during The Depression when almost every mother had to sew to keep their family in clothes.

So, a thimble was always available, easy to hide, and not a terrible loss if it got lost or some clumsy boy stepped on it, squashing it.

One person is chosen to hide the thimble while everyone else closes their eyes so they can't see where the "IT" puts it.

At the count of "twenty" everyone would open their eyes and start searching for that thimble.

Whoever finds the thimble gets to be the "IT" and so earns the right to hide it for the next round.

—Jennifer Miller

XXXVI

LONDON BRIDGE

 ondon Bridge can be played with four or more players. Two of the players face each other, and hold their joined hands up like a bridge. The other players walk single file in between the two bridge people, and under their arms. While they are doing all this, everyone sings: *"London Bridge is falling down, falling down, falling down. London Bridge is falling down, My Fair Lady."*

When the words "My Fair Lady" are sung, the two bridge people put their joined hands down close to the ground. In this move the bridge people trap one of the players; whichever one is walking under the bridge at the time.

The bridge people then shake the person in the middle back and forth while singing; *"Take the key and lock them up, lock them up. Take the key and lock them up. My fair lady."* The bridge people then raise their hands and the whole thing starts all over again.

Alma, an eighty year old friend of my Grandma's told me about playing London Bridge back in 1922. She grew up in Bonaparte, Iowa on the banks of the Des Moines River. Back in those days all the children had to work at home and do their chores. Once the chickens were fed and the cows milked, they were allowed to play.

One summer afternoon, Alma and her cousins were playing London Bridge while her brother, Albert, played "fetch the stick" with their big collie dog.

All of a sudden, on the "My Fair Lady" who would be caught in the bridges arms but that dog!

Laddie, the dog, barked and licked them all over their faces. She loved the attention and must of thought the children were playing the game just for her.

After that the girls had to quit playing for a while because Laddie kept running under their arms just as "My Fair Lady" was sung.

Alma thinks, yet to this day, that Laddie knew that song well enough, and deliberately ran into the girls' arms just at the right time to get caught.

—*Jackie Bodman*

XXXVII

DROP THE HANKIE

 veryone playing Drop The Hankie stands in a circle facing the middle. One person who is chosen to be the "IT" has a hankie. The "IT" goes around the outside of the circle, and quietly drops the hankie behind someone. Then that person chases the "IT" around

the circle back to the spot where the hankie was dropped. If the "IT" gets tagged, he or she has to go into the middle of the circle, called "the pot," The person that tagged the "IT" becomes the new "IT". The person in the pot has to stay there until another "IT" gets tagged.

One time, back in 1939, my Grandma was playing "Drop the Hankie" and got put in the pot fifteen times in just thirty minutes. Grandma was embarrassed and if that wasn't bad enough; she even got in trouble with her mother because of having a dirty hankie.

It's general agreed in the town of Grandview, Iowa that her fifteen times in the pot in thirty minutes was a Grandview record.

As far as we can figure out, that record stands yet today.

Grandma says it wasn't much fun setting that record since she really got it from her mother for that dirty hankie.

We don't know anything about what the record
is in Grandview, or anywhere else, for the dirtiest
hankie.

—*Amberly Lessenger*

XXXVIII

RING A ROUND THE ROSIE

ack in 1937, Miss Jenkins and her students made a rose garden at the rural Plesant Hill School near Willmathsville, Missouri. This was a whole school project. Today it would be considered a part of the study of plants, but in those days there was not special science class, and Miss Jenkins probably

thought it would be a good learning experience for her thirteen students in the little one room school where she taught.

The rose garden was in the front yard of the school where everyone passing by could see it. Almost every morning during the nice weather the younger children would make a circle around the

roses and tell each other stories. After that they would join hands and skip around the circle. One day Wilber, a fifth grader, made up a song to sing while they are circling the roses. It went something like this:

> *"Ring around the rosies,*
> *We don't blow our nosies.*
> *Last one down is a chicken."*

The last student to squat on the "down" part had to cluck like a chicken. The kids would take turns singing the verse, substituting different animals like goose so the children would have to honk; a cow so they would moo, and so forth.

Many different versions were made up by kids through the years. One popular verse made up by children living at Gulf Port, Illinois went like this:

(100)

"Ring around the lily pad,
Joe's not good, he's been bad.
Now we have to dunk him."

It wasn't too long before that verse had worked
it's way up and down the river from Gulf Port.

—*The Kids*

XXXIX

STEAL STICKS

ne day following a wind storm, my grandmother and her friend were picking up sticks on the school playground.

The girls decided to make their work a little more fun by seeing who could get the most sticks.

Grandma's friend, Fran, was getting jealous because my grandma was getting more sticks so she sneaked over and took three out of my grandma's pile.

To get back at her, my grandma stole three of Fran's sticks.

This stealing of each other's sticks went on until my grandma won because she had ended up talking all of Fran's sticks.

Grandma and Fran like to believe they were the inventors of "Steal Sticks". Whether so or not, they enjoyed many hours of mixing work with fun picking up willow sticks from the rural Washington school playground along the Iowa River.

—Stephani Bonnichsen

XL

CHALK THE ARROW

halk The Arrow has two team leaders and any number of players. The leaders pick their team by closing their eyes and turning their backs to the other players. One leader calls out a number, thereby getting the kid who has that number of fingers pointing up in the air.

One team covers their eyes and counts to one hundred while the others go in a group to hide. The leader of the hiding team draws an arrow on the sidewalk with chalk showing which way the team went to hide.

Each player on the team must hide somewhere off in the direction the arrow is pointing.

The other team sets out to find the hidden player, and especially search for the leaders. The hidden players work their way back to base to be "safe."

If anyone is caught they are taken back and are "out".

If the leader of the hiding team makes it back to base without being caught, that team wins.

It was a cloudy Saturday afternoon in May one spring in Oquawka, Illinois where Joe and some friends were playing Chalk the Arrow with some friends in a vacant lot across from the empty feed store.

Sprinkles of rain had been falling almost all morning but the weather never seemed to stop Joe and the other town kids from playing Chalk The Arrow and other fun games outside in Oquawka.

Joe was the leader of the hiding team. Just as the search team started counting and Joe drew an arrow in the direction of his hiding friends, there was a cloud burst.

As the rain suddenly started to come down in buckets, Joe finished the arrow and scurried off to join his friends inside the old feed store.

The drenched counting team reached one hundred, raced to look for the arrow, but couldn't find a trace of it. Where was it? What direction did those kids go to hide?

The down pour had washed the chalked arrow away just like an eraser will clean a blackboard.

The storm didn't let up, but the half-drowned searchers soon gave up and slopped on home.

The next day Joe and his team bragged all over school about how they were the Oquawka World Champion Chalk-The-Arrow players.

Between sneezes, the still chilled searching team tried to argue them out of their championship.

—*Brian Boka*

XLI

MIDNIGHT-STARLIGHT

idnight-Starlight is a game to be played of an evening after it's dark outside.

One person is "IT" and everyone agrees on something to be the base. The old iron yard gate used to be the favorite place for base when my mother was a kid.

First, the "IT" counts to one hundred, then chants "Midnight, Starlight, I hope to see a ghost tonight."

While the "IT" is counting, all the other players hide outside around the house and yard. After counting, the "IT" will go and try to find the others before they can sneak back to base without being caught.

If the "IT" cannot find everyone, he or she will yell, "All'e, All'e, in Free."

One time my mother, her brother and some of their friends were all playing Midnight-Starlight at their house. They were on their last game of the evening and everyone except my mother's little brother had either been caught or made it back to base.

The "IT" kept yelling "All'e, All'e in free", but the little boy still didn't come to the base.

After more yelling and searching, the children finally told the grown-ups about the missing boy.

Lanterns were lit, and the search began. After what seemed like forever, Grandma shouted, "Here he is, asleep in the hammock."

The little kid didn't even wake up when his mother took him in the house, to bed.

—*Brian Boka*

XLII

MAKING MUD PUDDLES

ack in the 1930's, store bought toys were few and far between. Most of the kids growing up in Bible Grove, Missouri were lucky if they owned even one such rarity. Times were tough, so the children had to dream up their own fun things to do.

Making Mud Puddles was one of the favorites. The children would get down into the muddy ditches or creek beds, pull off their shoes and pick out their special spot. Then, each would proceed to prance around until they started to work up some mud with their feet.

Whoever could make the most or the largest mud puddle in a designated length of time was the winner for the day.

Since none of the kids owned a watch back then, they used something from nature to determine the stopping point for each game. They might say the game would be over by the behavior of the cattle grazing in the pasture nearby. When the old Brown

Swiss got to the pond or the herd all passed the big oak tree could be their time regulator for making mud puddles. Many times an unsuspecting cow, simply by reaching for a tuff of bluegrass instead of a dandilion clump would determine the outhouse of a contest.

—*Rebecca Erwin Wilson*

XLIII

CONCENTRATION

All you need to play concentration is a group of people who can snap their fingers.

Players sit in a circle with one person picked to start the game. The starter begins by slapping his or her leg once, clapping once, snapping fingers on the left hand, and then on the right.

After this, the whole group joins in the sequence. They begin by the starter saying their own name on the first snap with their left hand and the name of someone else in the circle when they snap with their right hand.

Next, the person whose name was called by the starter on the right hand snap does the same thing. This game keeps going until someone gets out by not thinking of a name or getting off beat. The game is over when there are only two players left and then one of them makes a mistake.

(113)

Years ago, the kids in Boonville, Missouri enjoyed combining the game of Concentration with water fun on the banks of the Missouri River. Wearing their swimming suits, they would go down to the river and begin playing Concentration.

The last two players in the game got to throw the others in the river, and dunk them. The girls usually played that version of the game since the boys were always too anxious to get on with the swimming.

Concentration could be played around the fireplace or kitchen table of a winter evening, too, of course.

—Tracy Fultz

XLIV

DUCK 'EM

uck 'Em is a game that started out with the old fashioned swing, the kind with a piece of rope and a board to sit on.

One player sits in the swing while the other player pushed on the seat until it gets to going as high as it can without spilling the swinger out onto the ground.

Sometimes the game of Duck-Em would end before it really got started as a miscalculation would be made and the swinger would end up with the wind knocked out of him.

After the swing gets

to going good, the player on the ground tries to tag the person in the swing from the front while the person in the swing tries to tag the one on the ground with his foot. The first person to tag and other ten times is the winner.

One lazy summer afternoon Edna and George were playing Duck 'Em at their folks' place on the Cedar River near Moscow, Iowa.

Edna had been the swinger for two games and refused to trade place with George. It didn't take long for the game to turn into an arguement, what with George getting more and more upset.

The tags were getting rougher and harder. They were actually more like hits than just tags.

Suddenly, Edna's foot hit George so hard that he went rolling across the yard and down over the river bank.

With a sudden change of heart (helped along with visions of a good spanking) Edna jumped down from the swing to see if her little brother was hurt or had drowned.

It didn't take Edna long to find out that he was still alive, for as she peered over the bank, a big old glob of mud caught her right in the face.

Edna and George weren't what you'd call real good friends that day.

—*Garren Noll*

XLV

KING OF THE HILL

ing Of The Hill is played with four or more people.

It's not a complicated game at all. It's real simple. All the players stand at the top of a small hill. The object is for each person to try to push the others off the hill.

Once a person loses his balance and falls or rolls down the hill, the must stay there until the game is over. The last person standing on top of the hill is the winner, and is declared the "King of The Hill."

An older neighbor of my Aunt's told me about her playing King of the Hill when she was a little girl.

Her name was Harriett, and she grew up pretty much of a river rat kid down along the Ohio.

Harriett recalled the fun she and his cousins had with this game on her grandmother's cellar hill. In those days, folks had fruit cellars, or caves, instead of basements.

They would play for hours on the back side of the mound over the fruit cellar. Harriett's grandmother always had dark red hollyhocks growing in front on the crest above the old wooden door.

 Unfortunately, the geese that she also had, used to like to lay in the shade of those hollyhocks, and made it kind of messy in there.

One time Harriett's cousin, Norma, got pushed and rolled down the hill right into those hollyhocks and a fresh pile of goose doo doo.

That was the day that Norma learned to watch which way she rolled when she got pushed off of that little hill.

—Jackie Bodman

XLVI

CRACK THE WHIP

or Crack The Whip, you had to have six or more players.

Everyone holds hands in a line and the leader starts running, holding onto the next person's hand. He'll swerve back and forth like some sort of human serpent.

As the momentum grows, the last people in the chain of players will have a hard time hanging on, and will usually be whipped off the line, laughing at the same time.

My father and Uncle Rich were really good at this game. They were both good, stout leaders, especially Uncle Rich who used to milk ten cows by hand every morning and every night. He was almost always chosen to be the leader of "crack the whip."

Uncle Rich and his friends played this game as children at the old camping grounds north of Wapello, Iowa, along the Iowa River.

One time Uncle Rich cracked the whip so hard that over half of the fifteen kids went flying off.

The force threw them into the slimy mud by the edge of a cornfield. Almost every spring the Iowa River would flood the fields in that spot.

When the water would go back into the river banks, all that would be left would be slick slimy mud.

The kids would get so covered with the gooey stuff that they looked like mud mummies. Of course, it wouldn't do for just those particular kids to be all muddy, so they would chase the clean ones in an effort to get them just as dirty.

So, while that river mud would always worry the children's fathers about how they would get a crop in the field that year, it didn't bother the kids. For them, that mud was just lots and lots of fun.

—*Garren Noll*

(122)

XLVII

BARREL RACES

ack in 1937, as the story is told, Chester and Leo were looking for something exciting to do that hot summer afternoon before evening chores had to be done.

These two boys would be six graders at the Letts Elementary school when it started in less than a month. They both knew that the time for having fun would be drawing to a close, and they best be on with it full tilt for the rest of the summer.

It was simply a matter of honor, of course, for the pair to have as much fun, and to collect as many bruises and cuts as possible before school.

So, it didn't take long for an idea to strike the pair when they spied a couple old barrels behind the school house.

Each boy picked out his barrel, stood on it, and made it roll with his feet. After a while, barrel walking turned into barrel racing.

And racing on level ground proved to be too tame, so they headed for the old sledding hill. After all, if it would work for a sled in the winter, why wouldn't it work for a barrel in the summer?

But, it wasn't the same. Gravity worked pretty well for the boys in a sled, but was a lot tricker while trying to stay on top of a barrel that seemed to come alive on a hill.

It soon became clear that the best use for the feet was to slow the rolling barrel down rather than to make it move forward as it had been on the level.

Soon it wasn't who was going to win the race, but rather . . . who could stay on the longest?

But boys were pretty good at picking up such useful talents as riding a barrel down a hill, and it wasn't long until they were good enough to consider a race.

The contest started, and they stayed pretty even until about half way down the hill when Leo's barrel rolled over a mud clod.

Chester came down the hill slower, but stayed on top his vehicle. When he got to the bottom and could look up to find his friend, he found Leo was nowhere to be seen.

A series of blurbs and gasps led Chester to check out the drainage ditch there along the side of the road.

And, there was Leo, crawling up out of the water filled ditch, bringing about half of it up with him in his stomach and lungs.

All, in all, the boys considered it a pretty good race.

—Sam Langstaff

XLVIII

JACKS

 o play Jacks you need two or more players, ten metal jacks, and a rubber ball. And, you start out by scattering the jacks out on the floor.

To begin, a player throws up his rubber ball and while it is still in the air, quickly grabs a jack. Then he lets the ball bounce only once before catching it. If the ball bounces more than once the player has to put all his jacks back down on the floor.

Each time you throw the ball up, you have to pick up one more jack than you did the time before. The first player that runs out of jacks wins.

One day, a long time ago, my mother was playing jacks with some friends in her grandmother's kitchen. Leula, a friend, of Mom's, got so mad that she lost that she bounced the rubber ball as hard

as she could. The ball bounced on the kitchen counter, and landed in Great Grandma's big pot of bean soup.

Everybody scrambled to view the boiling pot of soup. Afraid of what Great-Grandma would say, they stood wide-eyed and silent.

Everything was alright, though, when Great-Grandma scooped the ball out and laughingly said, "Those beans needed some seasoning anyway."

—*Melissa Gage*

XLIX ᵢ

KICK THE CAN

ick The Can is played with four or more players and an old tin container, such as an old coffee can.

One person is chosen to be the "IT". The "IT" puts one foot on the can, covers his eyes and counts slowly to fifteen.

While the "IT" is counting, the other players scatter and hide, just as they would if playing hide and seek.

When the "IT" finishes counting, he tries to find the hiding players. If one is found, that person must sit or stand by the can. If any player that has not been caught yet comes out of hiding, runs and kicks the can, the players that had previously been caught get to go free. The process then starts all over again.

Hazel, an elderly neighbor of mine, told me about kick the can. She grew up in the small town of Beecreek, Illinois. Beecreek is a nice little place along the Illinois River.

Hazel remembers playing Kick the Can as a child with other children in her class. They used an old baking soda can to play with back then because most everybody in town bought coffee in a sack.

—*Jackie Bodman*

L

WOODEN BOX HOCKEY

o play wooden box hockey, you need a rectangular wooden frame made out of 2x6's or whatever material is available. An additional board is nailed across the middle to divide the rectangle in half. Two four inch slots are cut in the middle section and one slot in each of the end boards. These slots are for the hockey puck to go through.

The game is usually played on a sidewalk, like one that goes out to the garden out behind the house.

The players begin by hitting their sticks to the sidewalk on their side of the box. Next they cross over and strike against the oppoent's stick in the center. This process is repeated, and on the third strike, both try to hit the puck.

Each player continues to keep the opponent from scoring while attempting to work the puck through

(131)

the end slot. Every time a goal is scored, the game is started over with the process of the sticks hitting the sidewalk, then each other. The first player to get ten goals is the winner.

My father and his brother played this game when they were kids. They usually had to start out by building the box, of course. They discovered that building the box was all part of the fun of a summer afternoon of playing "Wooden Box Hockey."

—*Jackie Bodman*

LI

SPIN THE BOTTLE

his game takes ten or more players so is best played at school, when lots of company comes, or some other time when lots of kids can get together.

The players should sit in a circle with one of them using a milk bottle as a spinner.

Before spinning the bottle, he or she must ask a question like "Who is the smartest?" or "Who has the biggest feet?" Then the player spins the bottle. When the bottle stops and points to someone, that is the player who has the biggest feet or is the answer to whatever question was asked. The person that the bottle points to now is the spinner and can ask the question.

My great grandmother remembers playing the game one day when she was a little girl. She spun the bottle too hard and it went out of control. That flying bottle hit another little girl who fell into a table and sent it sprawling across the room, finally tipping over, and dropping all kinds of stuff out onto the floor.

Grand-Grandmother got a good whipping for all that. Her mother was not only mad at the children for breaking things up, but also for playing the game in the first place. She said to was sinful.

The kids always wondered why that old lady thought that about such an innocent game.

—*Lindsey Lorber*

LII

OUR COOK DOESN'T LIKE PEAS

 his was a game used my many rural school teachers as a reward for the students getting all their homework done or for a perfect spelling paper.

All the players sit in a row. Then one sits in front of them and says to each one in turn: "Our cook doesn't like peas; what can you give her instead?"

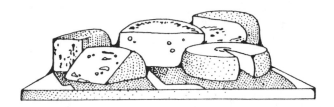

The first child may answer "Cheese" and that will suit the teacher, but the next one might say "potatoes" and that will not do, and he or she will have to pay a forfeit because the letter "P" comes in that word.

There is a catch to this as everyone, in the excitement of it all, tends to think that the vegetable "peas" is meant instead of the letter "P".

If a player fails to answer before the count of five, a forfeit is paid.

My Grandmother Doesn't Like Tea is played the same way.

—*The Kids*

LIII

BLACKBOARD RELAY

 lackboard Relay started in the one-room school house. It was usually played by students in grades six through eight. It was a bit too hard for the little ones, although some could take part in it except for when it came time to do the punctuation.

(137)

The players are seated in rows of equal numbers in each row. The last player in each row has a piece of chalk. On the teacher's signal to start, each of those children runs to the board, writes a word, then quickly returns to their seat, and gives the chalk to the person sitting in front of him.

The next player then runs forward, writes a word next to the first that makes sense with the first word, returns, and gives the chalk to the person sitting in front of him.

The game goes on like this until the last player runs forward, finishes the sentence, and punctuates it.

Then, that last player races back to his seat and raises his hand as the signal that his row is done.

Of course, in order for it to be an offical game of Blackboard Relay, it is necessary that there be lots of racing around, hollering and otherwise letting off steam.

After everybody is given a moment to rub their sore elbows from hitting the pencil sharpener, get their breath again, and get calmed down, the teacher figures up the scores.

Each team is awarded points for various things. There are, for example, up to five points for speed, five points for punctuation, five points for neatness,

and five points for spelling. In addition, points are given for writing and construction. The row that has the largest score wins the game.

Rural school teachers especially liked for their students to play this game because it served as a fun way to enrich the regular handwriting, grammer and spelling lessons.

—*The Kids*

LIV

CORN COB DARTS

To play corn cob darts you need a corn cob three or four inches long with both ends broken off.

Next, you gather (any way you can) three wing feathers from chickens or ducks.

(141)

The perils and pitfalls that a kid can get himself into while gathering feathers from unwilling chickens is a whole 'nother story.

The feathers should have a curve in them, and all three of them should be as much alike as is possible.

You stick the pointed and hard part of the feathers all into the white soft part of the corn cob.

 All that's left to do now is to choose a target. Just about anything can be used for that, even a circle in the ground.

The players take turns throwing the corn cob dart into the air toward the target. The player who hits the chosen target the most times is the winner.

One time when my father was a boy, he and his friend, Cliff, were playing corn cob darts. They had chosen the water bucket on Grandma's old hand pump well to serve as their target. Each of them had tossed their darts several times.

But, one time as they were retreiving their darts from around the bucket, their eyes fell on one of Grandma's cats there by the back door, lapping up leftover gravy from dinner.

The two boys looked at each other, neither one of them having to tell the other what they were thinking. One innocent cat and several corn cob darts all added up to the possibility for lots of fun without the two of them having to talk about it.

The cat was in trouble.

Well, actually, the cat wasn't really in trouble. In fact, the only one was Cliff.

My farthest throw at that cat bounced harmlessly off the pump handle. But Cliff wasn't so lucky. His smashed right into the glass window.

Sometimes chickens get their revenge in strange ways.

—*Garren Noll*

LV

LEAP FROG

Leap Frog is a game usually play-
outside with two or more people.

One person gets down on his knees,
or simply leans over while the person behind him puts his hands on
the first person's back and leaps over him.

Then, they continue taking turns doing this until they reach the end of the yard or they all decide to quit.

Years ago some boy scouts were playing leap frog at Crapo Park in Burlington, Iowa. They had leaped

their way across the fresh mown and trimmed grass, and were almost to the outdoor band shell when all of a sudden a big blue racer snake came slithering by them.

Up until then the boys had been talking about what tough scouts they were since they had been to Camp Eastman. After their visit from their long skinny friend, however, they stopped all that bragging.

From that time on for the rest of the day those boys didn't get but a few feet away from the scout master.

—*Joe Bunn*

LVI

MARBLES

o play marbles, draw a ring or circle in the dirt. Fifty or so marbles are put in the center of the ring. Each of the players have to put his share in that circle in order to play.

Each player has a big marble called a "shooter." When it's time for a player to shoot, he puts his shooter at the edge of the ring and flicks it with his forefinger. The marbles knocked outside the ring by the shooter belong to that person.

Players take turns shooting until all marbles are knocked out of the circle. The object of the game is to have gotten more marbles out than you put in.

Joe, a friend of mine who lives in a nursing home now told me about his childhood experiences playing marbles. In 1940 he and his family were at a family reunion at a little clearing on the Skunk River near Fort Madison, Iowa. Joe and his cousins had been busy skipping rocks and running in the timber when his mother called "Quiet Time".

"Quiet Time" was the signal that the children had to do something restful so that they would be fit to live with when they came to the table cloth spread there on the grass to eat.

So, the boys started a game of marbles to occupy their time for the half hour until dinner time. They picked a small dry sandbar right there at the edge of the Skunk River.

It was Joe's turn to shoot and there was but one solitary marble left in the ring.

Tension was mounting because Joe and his cousin, Glen, were tied for first place. Whoever got that last marble would be able to lord it over the other one the rest of the reunion.

Joe positioned the big green shooter carefully for his final attempt.

"Get 'er, Joe," urged a bystander.

With a flick of his thumb, Joe's shooter seemed to disappear from sight as it flashed forward toward that last marble.

Then, almost as quickly that marble in the ring shot out of the circle where Joe grabbed it up.

But, it wasn't over yet. With a long lazy arc, Joe's

(149)

precious green shooter took off out over the water and disappeared in the waters of the Skunk River.

The shooter was gone, as was Joe's short-lived victory. That bunch of boys declared Glen the winner of the match.

—Brian Boka

LVII

STREETS AND ALLEYS

hildren, to play this game, have to line up in several rows like checker-board men on a checker-board. They hold their arms out so their finger-tips almost touch.

With this arrangement, a person can run down between a couple of rows, but not from one row to another.

But, an interesting things happens when all the children turn a quarter turn. What used to be the "streets" are blocked, and rows called "Alleys" are made so the children running within the "checker-board" can now run the direction they could not before.

A person who is "IT" has to chase another person down the rows. A leader will call out "Street!" or "Alley", thus causing the "checkerboard men" to pivot back and forth, opening aisles one way, then another, as the extended arms made new circumstances in an instant.

One day, a long time ago a classmate of my Mother's was playing Streets and Alleys with his friends near what used to be called the New Boston

Ferry Landing at New Boston, Illinois on the Mississippi River. He was "IT", and the leader called "Alleys".

This young fellow was getting ready to turn, but when the passageway changed, he couldn't. He tried to stop, but instead slipped in the mud and fell right into the water by the boat landing. He had to do some real fast talking when he got home because his mother didn't let him play near the river.

His story about being pushed into a mud puddle didn't get far since they had been having a drought in the New Boston area at the time.

—*Jennifer Miller*

LVIII

ANDY OVER

ndy Over was played by dividing a group into two sides, usually by having a captain for each side. The captains would get to choose up sides.

A ball would be thrown over the roof of the little one room school building. Country schools were a lot smaller than elementary schools are today. That allowed for using the building in playing the game.

With teams on opposite sides of the school, the ball was thrown back and forth over the roof. When one player threw the ball, he or she would yell "Andy Over" and someone on the other side would try to catch it as it came down on that side.

After making the throw, the tossing team would run to the other side and try to tag the person who caught the ball. If that player was tagged, then he had to join the other team and become one of its members.

When the ball was thrown, and it failed to clear the peak of the roof, the throwing team would yell "Pigtail". This would let the catching team know that the ball didn't make it over.

The game continued this way, with each team alternating throwing, catching and tagging. The team with the most players when recess was over was declared the winner.

—*The Kids*

LIX

SNATCH BALL

ne day back in 1935, Mrs. Bonnichsen was getting her little rural school students ready for recess games. She had them sitting in a circle under the biggest oak tree on the playground.

They were all there, that is, all except for Randy who was being difficult and declared his intent to play football instead of circle games.

Randy had already been in trouble that morning for sticking Norma Jean's pigtail in the ink well, so Mrs. Bonnichsen's patience with him had about run out anyway. She told Randy to join in with the others and to get in the middle of the circle. She had already set his football in there to entice him into doing what she wanted.

Just about then John, another mischievous one, jumped up and grabbed Randy's football from the center of the circle.

Soon a new game had developed. Anyone who could snatch the ball from the center of the circle without being tagged by the one guarding it would become the new person in the middle. That person became the new center guard and assumed the responsibility of guarding the ball by tagging those who tried to snatch it.

So, that recess, without even trying, the children in Mrs. Bonnichsen's school invented a new game. The students were allowed to continue playing their new game of Snatch Ball and all were happy, even Randy.

—*Stephani Bonnichsen*

IX

ONE OLD CAT

his game uses a softball and a bat. You also need a place to call the pitcher's box, a home plate and first base. You also need four or more players, kids who have escaped the chores that kids had to do on Saturday mornings since this is one of those rarin'-to-go Saturday morning games.

You know you can have a regular softball game when you got enough kids to fill all the places, but if you've only got four, ONE OLD CAT will do.

The four gotta-haves are batter, pitcher, catcher, and fielder. If there are more refugees from wood cuttin' and gras mowin' you can use 'em for second fielder, third fielder, and so forth.

The players can decide on such softball rules that fit their 'druthers, or at least the 'druthers of whoever owns the bat and ball.

(157)

Each player scores for him or her-self alone when batting.

The batter scores by hitting a fair ball and running to first base and back to home plate without being put "out". The batter may be put "out" by another player's catching a fly, by having a foul ball, the catcher's tagging home plate with the ball before the runner touches the plate, or by making three strikes.

When the batter is put "out", the players rotate positions; the batter becomes the fielder; the first fielder becomes the pitcher; the pitcher becomes the catcher; and the catcher becomes the new batter. Some times the game is called "Work-Up."

No one was any more of an expert at this game than my Grandpa Erwin. He would round up all eight of us grandkids together on a Saturday morning and the game would be underway.

Everyone played, including Grandpa and even my little sister Reta. Excuse me, Grandpa called her "Dottie Dripple". He had a special nickname for each one of us.

Oh, how he loved us and the game of baseball. No one ever dare mention any team other than the St. Louis Cardinals because, in his eyes, they were the greatest.

Grandpa died in 1964 but, how I cherish the memories of "One Old Cat" and "Work-Up". I can still see the pride beaming from his face when one of us would make a good slide, catch or complete a difficult play around the roaming cats of Grandma's flower bed.

—*The Teacher*

EPILOGUE

Some were old and some were new, but the children in America's heartland enjoyed 'em all.

While Leap Frog might not have been very hi-tech and London Bridge didn't plug in anywhere or come with batteries, the children in the schoolyards and vacant lots of Mid-America had lots of fun with them years ago.

There was Two-Square-Four-Square, Whirl A Button, Blind Man's Bluff, and Statue Tag. There were Boxes, Ice Block Sliding and Simon Says.

If you'd care for a little trip into your own past, the ticket is in your hands right now.

Need a Gift?

For

- Shower • Birthday • Mother's Day •
  • Anniversary • Christmas •

Turn Page For Order Form
(Order Now While Supply Lasts!)

TO ORDER COPIES OF
Vacant Lot, School Yard, & Back Alley Games

Please send me _____ copies of **Vacant Lot, School Yard, & Back Alley Games** at $9.95 each. (Make checks payable to **QUIXOTE PRESS**.)

Name _____

Street _____

City _____ State _____ Zip Code ____

SEND ORDERS TO:

QUIXOTE PRESS
R.R. #4, Box 33B
Blvd. Station
Sioux City, Iowa 51109

TO ORDER COPIES OF
Vacant Lot, School Yard, & Back Alley Games

Please send me _____ copies of **Vacant Lot, School Yard, & Back Alley Games** at $9.95 each. (Make checks payable to **QUIXOTE PRESS**.)

Name _____

Street _____

City _____ State _____ Zip Code ____

SEND ORDERS TO:

QUIXOTE PRESS
R.R. #4, Box 33B
Blvd. Station
Sioux City, Iowa 51109

(164)

INDEX

Chapter Titles are
in
Capital Letters

A

B

E

F

G

H

J

K

L

M

(171)

T

U

V

W

(Continued on Next Page)

MISSISSIPPI RIVER PO' FOLK
by Pat Wallace . . . . paperback $9.95

STRANGE FOLKS ALONG THE MISSISSIPPI
by Pat Wallace . . . . paperback $9.95

THE VANISHING OUTHOUSE OF IOWA
by Bruce Carlson . . . . paperback $9.95

THE VANISHING OUTHOUSE OF ILLINOIS
by Bruce Carlson . . . . paperback $9.95

THE VANISHING OUTHOUSE OF MINNESOTA
by Bruce Carlson . . . . paperback $9.95

THE VANISHING OUTHOUSE OF WISCONSIN
by Bruce Carlson . . . . paperback $9.95

MISSISSIPPI RIVER COOKIN' BOOK
by Bruce Carlson . . . . paperback $11.95

IOWA'S ROAD KILL COOKBOOK
by Bruce Carlson . . . . paperback $7.95

HITCH HIKING THE UPPER MIDWEST
by Bruce Carlson . . . . paperback $7.95

IOWA, THE LAND BETWEEN THE VOWELS
by Bruce Carlson . . . . paperback $9.95

GHOSTS OF SOUTHWEST MINNESOTA
by Ruth Hein . . . . paperback $9.95

ME 'N WESLEY
by Bruce Carlson . . . . paperback $9.95
(Stories about the homemade toys that farm children made and played with around the turn of the century.)

SOUTH DAKOTA ROAD KILL COOKBOOK
by Bruce Carlson . . . . paperback $7.95

GHOSTS OF THE BLACK HILLS
by Tom Welch . . . . paperback $9.95

Some Pretty Tame, But Kinda Funny Stories About Early DAKOTA LADIES-OF-THE-EVENING
by Bruce Carlson . . . . paperback $9.95

Some Pretty Tame, But Kinda Funny Stories About Early IOWA LADIES-OF-THE-EVENING
by Bruce Carlson .... paperback $9.95

Some Pretty Tame, But Kinda Funny Stories About Early ILLINOIS LADIES-OF-THE-EVENING
by Bruce Carlson .... paperback $9.95

Some Pretty Tame, But Kinda Funny Stories About Early MINNESOTA LADIES-OF-THE-EVENING
by Bruce Carlson .... paperback $9.95

Some Pretty Tame, But Kinda Funny Stories About Early WISCONSIN LADIES-OF-THE-EVENING
by Bruce Carlson .... paperback $9.95

Some Pretty Tame, But Kinda Funny Stories About Early MISSOURI LADIES-OF-THE-EVENING
by Bruce Carlson .... paperback $9.95

THE DAKOTA'S VANISHING OUTHOUSE
by Bruce Carlson .... paperback $9.95

ILLINOIS' ROAD KILL COOKBOOK
by Bruce Carlson .... paperback $7.95

OLD IOWA HOUSES, YOUNG LOVES
by Bruce Carlson .... paperback $9.95
(Stories about old houses in Iowa and young loves they have known.)

TERROR IN THE BLACK HILLS
by Dick Kennedy .... paperback $9.95

IOWA'S EARLY HOME REMEDIES
by various .... paperback $9.95

GHOSTS OF DOOR COUNTY, WISCONSIN
by Geri Rider........................ paperback $9.95

THE VANISHING OUTHOUSE OF MISSOURI
by Bruce Carlson ....paperback $9.95

JACK KING vs. DETECTIVE MacKENZIE
by N. Bell............................paperback $9.95

RIVER SHARKS & SHENANIGANS
(tales of riverboat gambling of years ago)
by N. Bell............................paperback $9.95

TALES OF HACKETT'S CREEK
(1940s Mississippi River Kids)
by D. Titus...........................paperback $9.95

LOST & BURIED TREASURE OF THE MISSISSIPPI RIVER
by N. Bell............................paperback $9.95

ROMANCE ON BOARD
by Helen Colby ....paperback $9.95

UNSOLVED MYSTERIES OF THE MISSISSIPPI
by N. Bell............................paperback $9.95

TALL TALES OF THE MISSISSIPPI RIVER
by D. Titus...........................paperback $9.95

TALL TALES OF THE MISSOURI RIVER
by D. Titus...........................paperback $9.95

MAKIN' DO IN SOUTH DAKOTA
by various ....paperback $9.95

TRICKS WE PLAYED IN IOWA
by various ....paperback $9.95

OLD MISSOURI HOUSES, NEW LOVES
by Bruce Carlson ....paperback $9.95

LET'S GO DOWN TO THE RIVER 'AN . . .
by various ....paperback $9.95

EARLY WISCONSIN HOME REMEDIES
by various ....paperback $9.95

EARLY MISSOURI HOME REMEDIES
by various ....paperback $9.95

MY VERY FIRST . . .
by various . . . . paperback $9.95

101 WAYS FOR IOWANS TO DO IN THEIR NEIGHBOR'S PESKY DOG WITHOUT GETTING CAUGHT
by B. Carlson . . . . paperback $7.95

SOUTH DAKOTA ROADKILL COOKBOOK
by B. Carlson . . . . paperback $7.95

A FIELD GUIDE TO IOWA'S CRITTERS
by B. Carlson . . . . paperback $7.95

A FIELD GUIDE TO MISSOURI'S CRITTERS
by B. Carlson . . . . paperback $7.95

MISSOURI'S ROADKILL COOKBOOK
by B. Carlson . . . . paperback $7.95

A FIELD GUIDE TO ILLINOIS' CRITTERS
by B. Carlson . . . . paperback $7.95

MINNESOTA'S ROADKILL COOKBOOK
by B. Carlson . . . . paperback $7.95

REVENGE OF THE ROADKILL
by B. Carlson . . . . paperback $7.95

THE MOTORIST'S FIELD GUIDE TO MIDWEST FARM EQUIPMENT
(misguided information as only a city slicker can get it messed up)
by B. Carlson . . . . paperback $7.95

ILLINOIS EARLY HOME REMEDIES
by various . . . . paperback $9.95

GUNSHOOTIN', WHISKEY DRINKIN', GIRL CHASIN' TALES OUT OF THE OLD DAKOTA TERRITORY
by Netha Bell . . . . paperback $9.95

WYOMING'S ROADKILL COOKBOOK
by B. Carlson . . . . paperback $7.95

(177)

MONTANA'S ROADKILL COOKBOOK
by B. Carlson . . . . paperback $7.95

SHE CRIED WITH HER BOOTS ON
(tales of an early Nebraska housewife)
by M. Walsh . . . . paperback $9.95

SKUNK RIVER ANTHOLOGY
by Gene "Will" Olson . . . . paperback $9.95

101 WAYS TO USE A DEAD RIVER FLY
by B. Carlson . . . . paperback $7.95

I-GOT-FUNNER-THINGS-TO-DO-THAN-COOKIN' COOKBOOK
by Louise Lum . . . . paperback $11.95

IOWA, A JOURNEY IN THE PROMISE LAND
by K. Yoder . . . . paperback $16.95

GUN SHOOTIN', WHISKEY DRINKIN', GIRL CHASIN', FROG STOMPIN' TALES Out of the LAND of the LAKES
by Netha Bell . . . . paperback $9.95

GUN SHOOTIN', WHISKEY DRINKIN', GIRL CHASIN', FROG STOMPIN' TALES Out of the OLD MISSOURI TERRITORY . . . . paperback $9.95

NUDE HUNTING IN ILLINOIS (Some things to think about while you're stompin' around Illinois in the buff.)
by Bruce Carlson . . . . paperback $7.95

A MOTORIST'S GUIDE TO ILLINOIS' WORST RESTAURANTS

by Bruce Carlson .... paperback $7.95

YOU KNOW YOU'RE IN ILLINOIS WHEN . . .

by Bruce Carlson .... paperback $7.95

WILD CRITTER COOKBOOK

by Bruce Carlson .... paperback $11.95

HOW US ITTY BITTY KIDS WOULD RUN A HOUSE IF WE HAD TO

by various .... paperback $7.95